Draw yourself with
a funny hairstyle.

Amazing
MAZE

the BiG RED activity book

Drawing, doodling,
activity-o-rama!

Hilarious hair

Complete these funny faces with some wacky hairdos.

Arthur needs to get to the castle. Fill the garden with a twisting, turning maze, and then give it to a friend to solve!

Super shield

Decorate this medieval shield with a design to scare off your enemies!

Add stickers and designs
to create your own
monster mask!

hole for string

hole for string

For extra fun, carefully cut out the mask and add a hole on the left
and right sides. Ask an adult to help you thread some string through
each hole, and tie a knot to secure it around your head. Make sure
the string is not too tight around your head or neck!

MONSTER

Decorate these scary monster faces and use them as inspiration for your mask.

Pirate Party

Can you spot the identical twin pirates?

Murky
mountains

Skull
rock

Forbidden
forest

X marks
the spot!

G'day
Australia!

Sydney Opera House

platypus

BBQ

ULURU

MATE

koala

kangaroo

Happy birthday!

Decorate this giant birthday cake with stickers, and add candles and amazing doodled details.

birthday   Happy

We all love you

Decorate this birthday card, and save it for your best friend's birthday.

HAPPY BIRTHDAY

Fold here

Cut out

Designed by

I drew you a birthday picture!

Happy birthday!

One good doodle deserves another! Fill this page with lots of different pets.

Family TREE

ME

Doodle your family
in the photo frames
on this tree or make up
a funny family!

Add faces to complete these
underwater creatures.

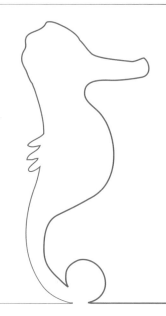

Now try doodling a diver
looking at these shells!

Doodle a seaside friend
for each of the animals.

wish you were here ...

It's vacation time! What will you pack in your suitcase?

Cut out and decorate this postcard, and then send it off to someone you know!

Stick
your
stamp
here!

BUBBLE WRITING

Practice writing your name
in cool bubble writing.

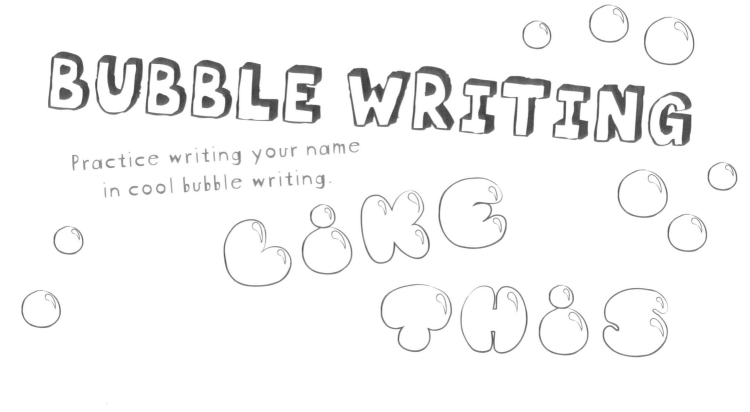

Enchanted FOREST

Who lives in this magical oak tree? Is it a fairy or a goblin ... or something else entirely?

Felix has lost his way in the enchanted forest. Which string should he follow to get home?

connect the dots ...

to discover who is in the jungle.

Who else can you see
hiding in the jungle?

How to draw

Step 1

Step 2

Step 3

Step 4

a penguin!

Practice drawing your
penguin pal here!

CRAZY ABC!

Create a crazy letter of your own!
Try using the first letter of your name.

_____'s

ROOM

Decorate and cut out this bedroom door sign.

Decorate a door sign

Dream house

Add stickers and doodles to the house below to create your perfect pad.

Fingerprint

farm

Create a doodle farm starting with your own fingerprint, and then add eyes, arms, legs, and anything else you can think of to make fantastic farmyard animals.

Once upon a time ...

What's gone wrong with this fairy tale?

Add stickers and drawings
to make this picture
even funnier!

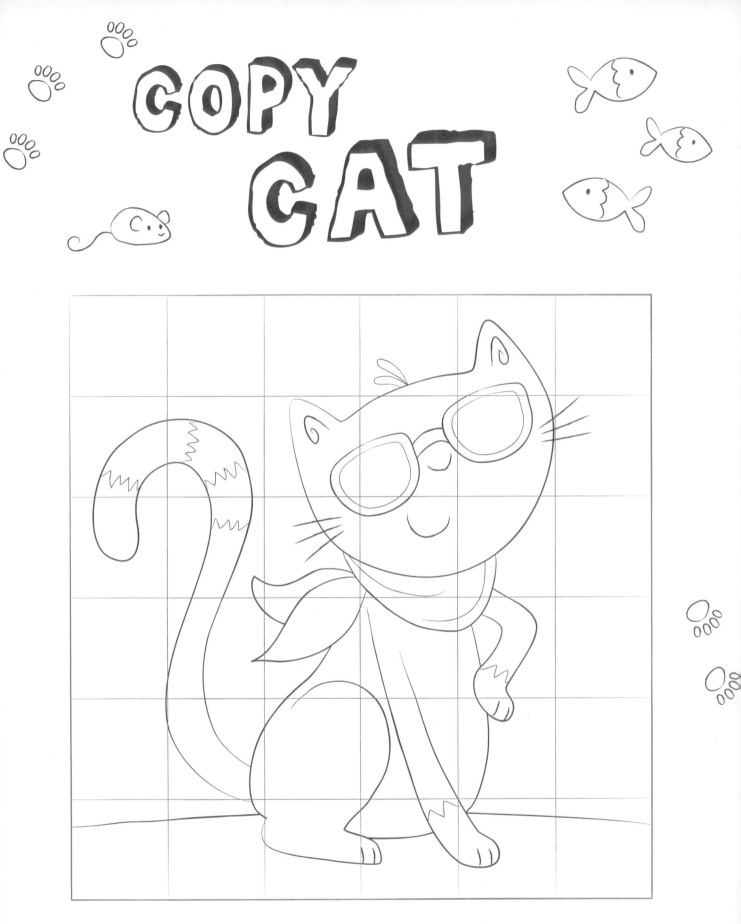

Use the grid to copy this
cool cat exactly.

cat

MEOW!

kitty

SWEET DREAMS

Doodle what these
siblings are dreaming ...

Can you complete this
sandcastle and design some
more on the opposite page?

Beach

challenge

Draw a face on the head below....

Now cover the head with a piece of paper and ask someone else to draw the body between the two lines.

Then cover the body and head and ask someone else to draw the legs. Take the paper away and look at the funny character you've made!

All mixed up!

Mirror mirror ...

Sit in front of a mirror and draw
yourself in this picture frame below.

TV star

If you were in a TV show,
what would it be about?
Doodle a scene on the TV screen.

IS it a BIRD?

Decorate this superhero's costume and give him a superhero name!

Never fear! _____ is here!

I'm HUNGRY!

The refrigerator is empty! Fill it up with some delicious food.

Build a BOX

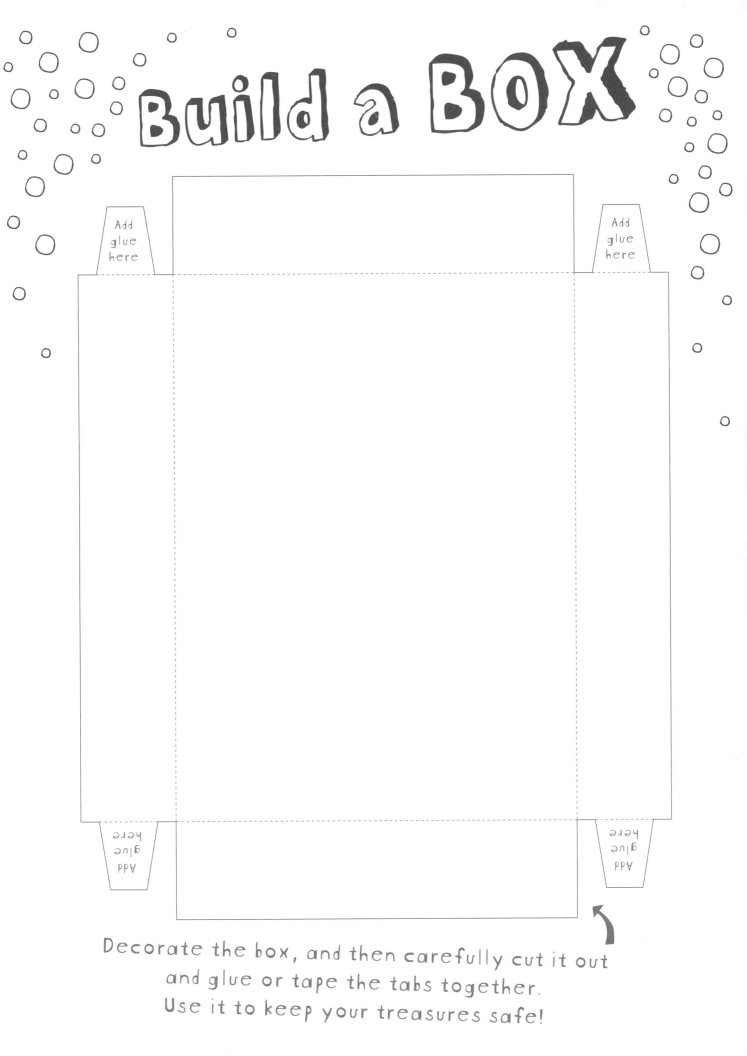

Add
glue
here

Add
glue
here

Add
glue
here

Add
glue
here

Decorate the box, and then carefully cut it out
and glue or tape the tabs together.
Use it to keep your treasures safe!

MODERN ART

Create a modern masterpiece by filling each section with a different pattern or design.

Cats
in hats

Give these cats
fantastic hats!

Going underground

Help the worm get to his home.

Wild weather

What's the weather forecast for this island? Fill in the map, and then use stickers to show what the weather is doing.

Do you like scary storms or random rainbows? Add the type of weather you like best to the scene.

Bake a cake

What are these cooks adding to their cake batter? Draw in the ingredients.

Broomstick basics

These magical students are learning to fly their broomsticks. Which one gets back to the school?

Making faces!

Lots of faces start as just a circle. Try drawing a person you know or a cute animal.

Plant pet

Complete this plant. Is it a beautiful buttercup or a vicious Venus flytrap?

I AM TALLER THAN ...

Customize your very own height chart!
Ask an adult to help you safely secure this
chart to a wall. Make sure you hang the chart
2 feet up from the ground.

Then, on the chart, write the date
next to your height as you grow!

5'7"

5'6"

HOW TO USE
Cut out the next five pages, fill them in, and stick them together.
Add glue here to secure this page to the next page.

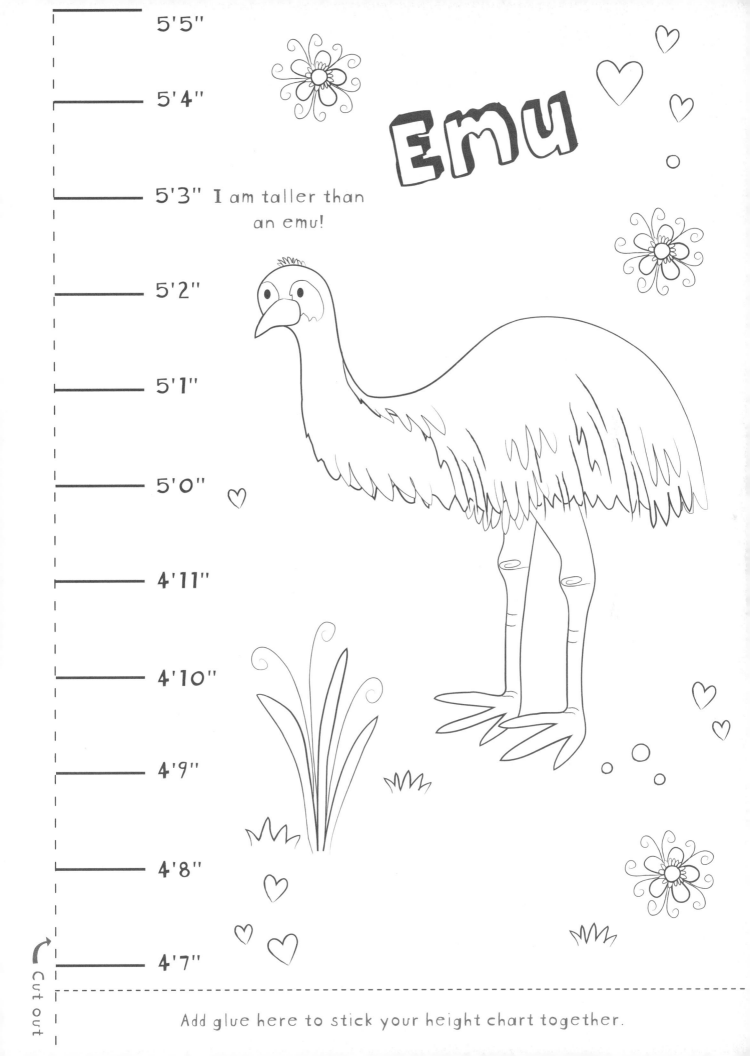

5'5"

5'4"

5'3" I am taller than
an emu!

Emu

5'2"

5'1"

5'0"

4'11"

4'10"

4'9"

4'8"

4'7"

Cut out

Add glue here to stick your height chart together.

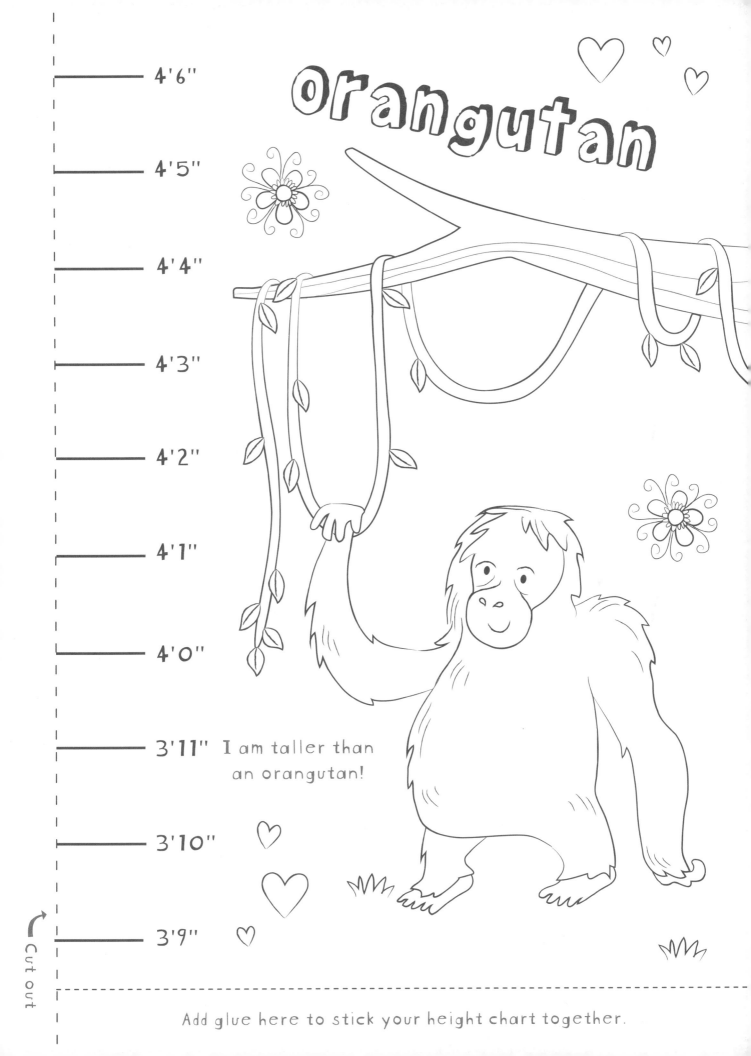

orangutan

4'6"

4'5"

4'4"

4'3"

4'2"

4'1"

4'0"

3'11" I am taller than
an orangutan!

3'10"

3'9"

Cut out

Add glue here to stick your height chart together.

3'8"

3'7" I am taller than an
emperor penguin!

Emperor penguin

3'6"

3'5"

3'4"

3'3"

3'2"

3'1"

3'0"

2'11"

Cut out

Add glue here to stick your height chart together.

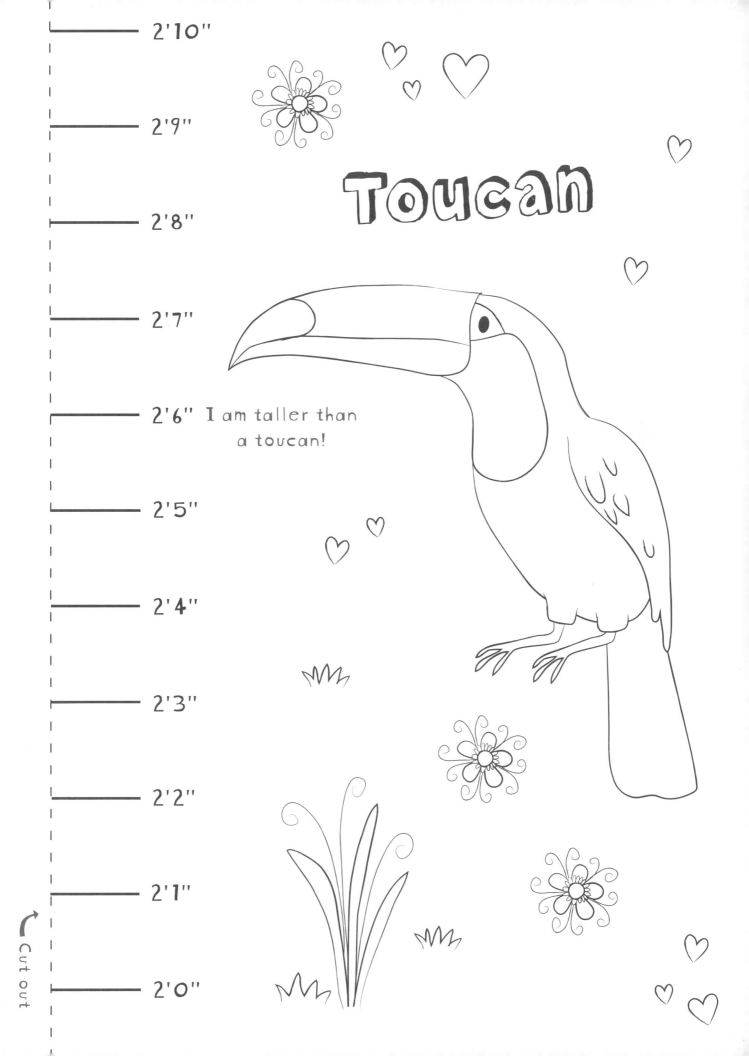

Toucan

2'10"

2'9"

2'8"

2'7"

2'6" I am taller than
a toucan!

2'5"

2'4"

2'3"

2'2"

2'1"

2'0"

Cut out

This is to
certify that

_____

is an

AWESOME
doodler!

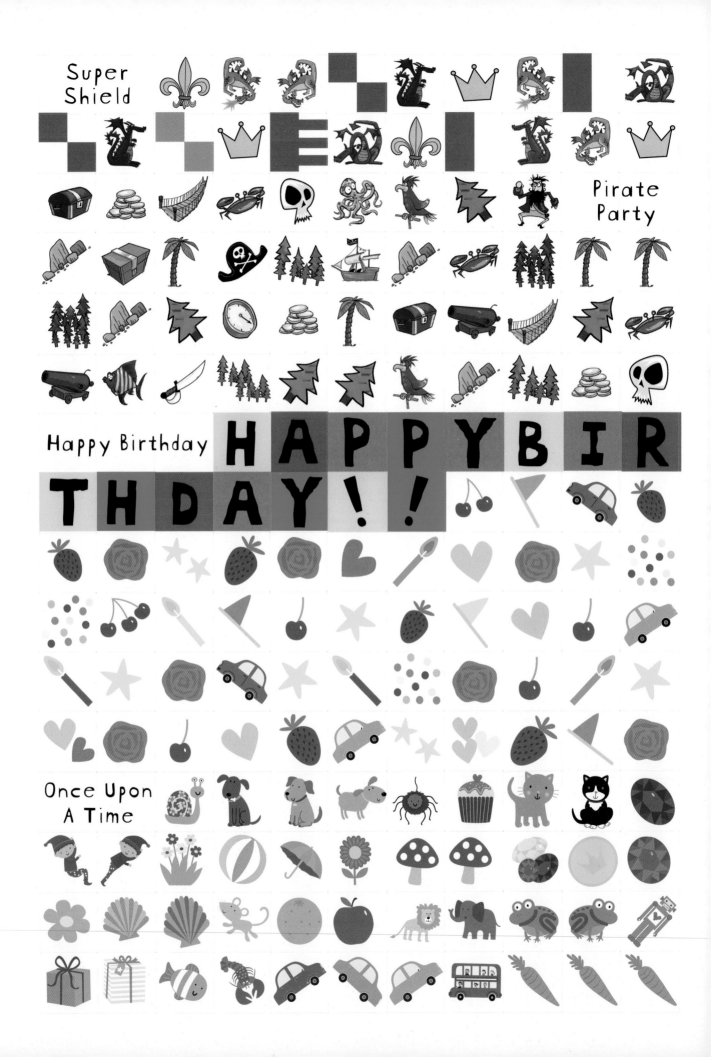

Super
Shield

Pirate
Party

Happy Birthday

Once Upon
A Time

Wild
Weather

STICKERS FOR FUN!

STICKERS FOR FUN!

STICKERS FOR FUN!

1 2 3 4 5 6 7 8 9

STICKERS FOR FUN!

STICKERS FOR FUN!